THE G.I. SERIES

American Indians in the U.S. Armed Forces, 1866–1945

For this portrait, taken in about 1870, Pawnee warrior Loots-tow-otts (Rattlesnake) of the Skidi band has donned an 1858-pattern infantry corporal's coat and holds an M1859 saber, probably a photographer's prop. His long hair and single feather combined with the regulation non-commissioned officer's coat reflect the Indian scout's precarious position as a bridge between two worlds. *(NSHS)*

THE G.I. SERIES

THE ILLUSTRATED HISTORY OF THE AMERICAN SOLDIER, HIS UNIFORM AND HIS EQUIPMENT

American Indians in the U.S. Armed Forces, 1866–1945

John P. Langellier

Greenhill Books
LONDON
Stackpole Books
PENNSYLVANIA

Greenhill Books

This book is dedicated to the memory of J. Edward Green III,
whose deep respect for the American Indian inspired this work.

American Indians in the U.S. Armed Forces,
1866–1945
First published 2000 by Greenhill Books, Lionel
Leventhal Limited, Park House, 1 Russell Gardens,
London NW11 9NN
www.greenhillbooks.com
and
Stackpole Books, 5067 Ritter Road, Mechanicsburg,
PA 17055, USA

British Library Cataloguing in Publication Data
Langellier, John P.
American Indians in the U.S. armed forces,
1866–1945. – (The G.I. series: the illustrated history
of the American soldier, his uniform and his
equipment; v. 20)
1. United States. Army – Indian troops 2. United
States – Armed Forces – Indians – History – 19th
century 3. United States – Armed Forces – Indians –
History – 20th century
I. Title
355'.008997

ISBN 1-85367-408-7

Library of Congress Cataloging-in-Publication Data
available

Designed by David Gibbons, DAG Publications Ltd
Layout by Anthony A. Evans, DAG Publications Ltd
Edited by Rachael Wilkie
Printed in Hong Kong

ACKNOWLEDGEMENTS AND ABBREVIATIONS

The author wishes to thank Richard LaMotte for the
custom art work, and the following individuals and
institutions:

AHS	Arizona Historical Society, Tucson, AZ
AMWH	Autry Museum of Western Heritage, Los Angeles, CA
BH	Bill Henry
CBF	Christian Barthelmess Family, Miles City, MT
CDG	Costume Designers' Guild
FHHM	Fort Huachuca History Museum, Fort Huachuca, AZ
GS	Glen Swanson
HF	MG Hugh Foster, Jr. USA (Ret)
HP	Herb Peck
ITC	Institute of Texan Culture, University of Texas, San Antonio, TX
JG	Jerome Greene
JNJ	Jacques Noel Jacobsen, Jr.
JO	James Osborne
JP	Joe Parr, Historic Framing and Collectibles, Ellicott City, MD
KC	Kurt Cox
KM	Kevin Mulroy, Ph.D.
LDS	Church Archives, The Church of Jesus Christ of Latter Day Saints, Salt Lake City, UT
MHS	Montana Historical Society, Helena, MT
NA	National Archives, College Park, MD
NSHS	Nebraska State Historical Society, Lincoln, NE
PS	Phil Spangenberger
SI	Smithsonian Institution, Museum of American History, Washington, DC
SISCA	Seminole Indian Scout Cemetery Association
USAMHI	U.S. Army Military History Institute, Carlisle Barracks, PA
WHM	William Hammond Mathers Museum, Wanamaker Collection, Indiana University, Bloomington, IN
WSM	Wyoming State Museum, Cheyenne, WY

AMERICAN INDIANS IN THE U.S. ARMED FORCES, 1866–1945

Early in 1775, the provisional Continental Congress invited the American Indian residents of Stockbridge, Massachusetts to join the rebellion against the British. Not until the following year was this recruitment expanded, when George Washington was permitted to enlist 2000 Native Americans for his army. The commander in chief recognized the potential of this force, which he thought could 'be made of excellent use as scouts and light troops'.

Great Britain likewise saw the benefits of drawing upon this considerable pool of manpower, which included many veteran warriors. In fact, Britain had long enjoyed strong economic, social, and even religious ties, with numerous Indian groups. As a result, George III mustered far more Indian allies than his rebellious subjects.

Nevertheless, those who rallied to the revolutionary cause, although in the minority, often did so with considerable resolve. For example, the Stockbridge contingent, which included Mohicans and other indigenous peoples, formed a colonial company that faced British dragoons. In a bitterly-fought battle in what is now New York City's Vancourtland Park, they sustained major casualties at the hands of his majesty's well-mounted horsemen. Similarly, half the Pequots serving in Connecticut regiments never returned home.

The Oneidas, who participated in campaigns from New York to New Jersey and Pennsylvania, also endured many losses. Indeed, symbolic of the rift between various Indian groups, one of the Oneida leaders fell at the Battle of Oriskany, an engagement that included a strong contingent of Mohawks who sided with the English.

This clash was not only characteristic of the breach between various Indian peoples, but also was indicative of the breakup of the longstanding Iroquois Confederation. For generations six 'nations' (Mohawks, Oneidas, Onondagas, Cayugas, Senecas, and later the Tuscaroras) had sat at the same council fires, therefore holding a strategic position that both the British and their American cousins courted for control of upper New York. Ultimately, the league disintegrated as former allies squared off into opposing camps.

During the War of 1812, when for a second time Great Britain and the United States faced each other, Indians again followed diverging courses. Some saw wisdom in the vision of the adroit Shawnee leader Tecumseh. He called for all Native Americans to band together against the United States. Joining the British in the Old Northwest, Tecumseh attempted to carry out this plan, while the Americans added other Indian people to their strength in a contest to control the region.

A similar story unfolded in the South, where the Creek nation of Alabama became so divided over allegiances that a civil war erupted between 'Red Sticks' and 'White Sticks'. Eventually Andrew Jackson entered the picture. With the aid of a regiment of Cherokees led by Creek native John McIntosh, and with the support of the Choctaws, 'Old Hickory' quelled the enemy. After his final victory at Horseshoe Bend, Jackson turned his attention to the British, again drawing upon Indian aid when he attacked Pensacola. Later, at the Battle of New Orleans, Jackson's Choctaw partners continued their support, standing alongside him as a mainstay on his left flank.

Despite their loyalty to the Americans by many Indians of the South, after the end of the War of 1812 widespread relocation to the West caused a number of former allies to be forced beyond the Mississippi. This included those who suffered during the 'Trail of Tears' that brought the 'Civilized Tribes' to far-away Indian Territory (Oklahoma).

Decades later, as strife tore the nation asunder, thousands of American Indians once more found themselves on diametrical paths. Not only were the whites of North and South fighting a civil war, but also many Indians became embroiled in this internecine clash. For instance, the Lumbee of North Carolina affiliated themselves with the Yankees against Rebel home guardsmen. Nearby, in South Carolina, the Catawba served as Confederate infantrymen. Further, those Cherokees who had been transplanted to Indian Territory splintered into northern and southern factions.

In all, some 20 000 Indians chose sides, and were present during nearly all the conflict from the battle of Wilson Creek, Missouri in 1861 to the siege of Vicksburg in 1864 and 1865. Indeed, General Ulysses S. Grant's military secretary, the Seneca sachem Ely S. Parker, transcribed the surrender document signed by Robert E. Lee to disband the Army of Northern Virginia. Afterward, Parker was promoted to the rank of brevet brigadier general of volunteers, and spent the next three years as Grant's aide-de-camp.

However, Appomattox did not mean the end of the fighting for all Southern units. Some of the last Confederate holdouts were Cherokees who, under the generalship of Stand Waite, their principal leader, remained in the field. Not until June 1865 did his command lay down their arms, at Doakville in the Choctaw Nation's portion of Indian Territory.

With Stand Waite's capitulation, and the subsequent end of the Confederacy, changes were wrought in various areas of American life. One of these began in 1866, with a more standardized incorporation of Native Americans into the military organization than had been customary beforehand. Prior to this time, quartermaster officers at individual posts hired Indians more or less as contract employees per the directives of their superiors. It was under this system, for example, that Major General Samuel Curtis had delegated authority during the Civil War to one of his subordinates, Frank North, to engage a group of Pawnees for duty on the Plains.

This ad hoc, localized recruitment gave way to a new method inaugurated by legislation in 1866. In that year, Congress authorized the president to enlist not more than 1000 Indians 'to act as scouts, who shall receive the pay and allowances of cavalry soldiers'. In spite of this, over the next three decades only about a third of this number actually were on duty at any given time. Diverse factors contributed to this situation, which caused certain military commanders to contract informal alliances or to sponsor raiding parties by one group against another.

Despite obstacles, many military leaders throughout the West actively recruited warriors for six-month stints of duty. Some of the scouts found the duty to their liking. They re-enlisted repeatedly, thereby constituting a cadre for field operations. So it was that, from the 1860s through the 1890s, scouts played an important role during more than a dozen significant campaigns waged on the western frontier.

For instance, in September 1872 the Modocs of Northern California faced increasing pressure from white incursion. Eventually, they fled to the region south of Tule Lake in the naturally fortified Lava Beds. In response, the military called upon another group of Indians living on the Warm Springs Reservation in Oregon. This was a composite of several different peoples who, soon after Robert E. Lee's surrender, had offered their services as trailers and combatants for white militiamen in operations against the Shoshones and Paiutes of the Great Basin. Now the Warm Springs braves contributed similar skills against the ill-fated Modocs. They, along with U.S. Army artillery and cavalry troops, eventually dislodged the Modocs, who were relocated to Quapaw Indian Agency in present-day Oklahoma.

Although the Modoc War received much press, the clash proved short-lived. That was not the case for the Apache wars, which raged for many years. During the so-called Geronimo campaigns, scouts – including many Apaches from opposing bands – furnished a valuable resource in the field. Brigadier General George Crook expressly championed a strategy that relied heavily upon scouts, based on his personal philosophy that it took 'diamond dust to polish a diamond' – in other words, the most promising means of subduing the Apache was with the aid of their own kind.

Sometimes this policy did not work according to plan, as witnessed in 1881 when some Apache scouts from Company A of the Sixth Cavalry allegedly turned their government-provided weapons on their fellow soldiers. This supposed mutiny at Cibecue Creek, Arizona Territory, led to the court martial of five of the scouts, three of whom were found guilty of murder and desertion in the face of the enemy. They were sentenced to death, and were hanged on 3 March 1882.

Despite the notoriety of the incident, the Cibecue affair was an aberration, although it did point out the rather ambivalent position of scouts during the Indian wars. For the most part the scouts served faithfully, but their role was drawing to a close. In the last decade of the nineteenth century, the cessation of hostilities in the West between Indians and whites brought about a new turn of events. On 19 March 1891, an army general order cut back the strength of the scouts to 150, with the Departments of the Dakota, Missouri and Platte being assigned twenty-five men each, with another fifteen to Texas and ten for the Department of Columbia. The remaining fifty allotments were retained for the Department of Arizona.

The same directive called for the conversion of Troop L in selected U.S. cavalry regiments, and Company I in certain U.S. infantry regiments, to consist of fifty-five American Indian enlisted men. The idea was to convert former nomadic warriors into disciplined regulars, who would be assimilated into the white culture as a result of their conversion into conventional soldiers. Thus, the Brule Lakotas, who once saw the whites as aggressors, became troopers in the Sixth Cavalry and foot soldiers in the Sixteenth Infantry. Likewise, Apaches, who formerly struck fear into the hearts of settlers of the Southwest, now marched under the standards of the Ninth, Tenth, Eleventh and Twelfth Infantry regiments, and the First Cavalry regiment. Cheyenne, Crow and others also put on the army blue, but only for a short time, as all the units were disbanded within a scant half-dozen years.

Most of the men returned to the status of civilians. A few had the opportunity to remain on the military rolls as scouts. When, in 1898, the Spanish-American War opened, some Indians even signed up for the First Volunteer Cavalry (the Rough Riders) bound for Cuba.

A generation later, as America entered World War I, the remnants of the Iroquois Confederation declared war on Germany because, as non-citizens, they viewed themselves as a distinct entity from the United States.

General Hugh Scott, who had closely watched the Indian Troop L and Company I experiment as a junior officer, was strong in his support for enlistment of Indians into the military. Higher authorities agreed. Over 6000 were drafted, and a similar number volunteered. Most entered the army, but 2000 went into the navy. Although not all of these Native American doughboys and bluejackets were shipped overseas, those who went could certainly find themselves in the thick of things. In such instances, deeply ingrained cultural traditions brought out the best in some of them. Most notably a Choctaw, Joseph Oklahombi, proved his mettle when he crossed over 200 yards of no man's land, making his way through entanglements of barbed wire and enemy fire to attack a German machine gun nest. Private

Oklahombi reached his objective and took 171 prisoners, thereby earning the *Croix de Guerre* from the impressed French high command.

Other Choctaws performed in yet another important way. Taking advantage of the obscurity of their language, some fourteen members of the Thirty-sixth Division were pressed into service as communication personnel. Dispersed throughout their regiment (the 142nd Infantry) they could communicate on field telephones without the bewildered forces of the Kaiser being able to determine what was being said. In order to accomplish their task, some improvisation was necessary. For example, they referred to battalions as grains of corn, and used the term 'big gun' for artillery, while 'little gun shoot fast' meant a machine gun.

After the Armistice was signed, the United States government recognized the role played by Native Americans in the 'war to end all wars'. In 1924 citizenship was granted at last to the nation's first residents, many of whom had taken up arms eagerly and distinguished themselves under fire.

Even as this new status was being bestowed, the U.S. military establishment shrank in size, particularly after the stock market crash of 1929. During the Depression that followed, few American Indians found a place in uniform, with some notable exceptions such as the Apache Scouts who continued to serve at Fort Huachuca, Arizona until 1943.

Then, late in the 1930s, American military might increased as the armed forces mobilized in response to international tensions. As part of preparedness, Congress passed a selective service act. Large numbers of Indian males registered, constituting one of the highest responses by any group in the nation. The fervor ran so high that, even before the draft, one-quarter of New Mexico's Mescalero Apaches enrolled, while nearby Navajos stood in line for hours, despite foul weather, to obtain their draft cards. A few even brought their own firearms to show they were ready to fight immediately. In 1942, the Navajos called a council which was attended by more than 50 000 Native Americans to demonstrate their commitment to the war effort. The head of the tribal council even proposed the raising of an all-Navajo regiment.

Further, every Chippewa man at Grand Portage, Michigan, volunteered for duty. Together with the Sioux and members of the former Iroquois Confederation, they came together with one voice. Despite the fact that they were no longer considered separate nations, they declared war on the Axis.

So it was that, just before the attack on Pearl Harbor, over 4000 American Indians had enlisted, representing one in every ten eligible men. More than 300 of this early group battled on in defense of Bataan and Corregidor. In the ensuing years, others answered the call, so that by VJ Day a third of all able-bodied Native American men aged 18-50 had entered the armed forces. There were 121 U.S. Coast Guardsmen, 1910 sailors, and 874 marines, while the remaining service members were scattered among U.S. Army ground and air forces. (Estimates run between 20 000-40 000, the higher figure taking into consideration those who joined from communities off the reservations.)

Certain units had high concentrations of American Indians. Most notably, the U.S. Army's Forty-fifth Infantry Division boasted over 2000 Indian businessmen, farmers and workers from Oklahoma and New Mexico, making up approximately one-fifth of the entire outfit. Appropriately, the division's shoulder sleeve insignia was a red lozenge with a gold thunderbird – a sacred symbol among some Indian peoples. From June 1943, when the unit landed in North Africa, through campaigns in Sicily, Italy, the Ardennes, and at last into Germany itself, the division spent a grueling 511 days in combat. This record brought special recognition to a Creek and a Cherokee in the unit. Lieutenant Ernest Childers and Technical Sergeant Van Barfoot each were presented with the Medal of Honor (six other Medals of Honor went to non-Indian members of the Forty-fifth) while many other Indian personnel in the division earned Bronze Stars for valor and Purple Hearts for wounds sustained in action.

Although the men of the Thunderbird Division gained many laurels, perhaps the most celebrated American Indians in World War II were the code talkers. Just like the military communication experts of World War I, their World War II counterparts realized the value of employing the complex, little-known Native American tongues. Some of the first men selected for this task were Comanches, who underwent training in the various aspects of army Signal Corps techniques and procedures. Then they launched into a program to convert their linguistic abilities into a cryptographic formula that could be broadcast openly with little fear that the enemy would decipher their messages. Posted to the Fourth Signal Company of the Fourth U.S. Infantry Division, these specialists worked with their officers to create an ingenious code. They used terms such as *posah-tai-vo* ('crazy white man') to

designate Adolph Hitler. When their vocabulary had no equivalent, as in the case where there was only one word for airplane, they expanded on the basic root and used the Comanche phrase that meant 'pregnant airplane' to indicate a bomber. Their baptism of fire came at Utah Beach, Normandy, when Comanche signalmen came ashore with their unit. From there, they went on through northern France, then into Luxembourg, where they participated in the Battle of the Bulge. The division commander ultimately commended them for their outstanding service.

While the Comanches were plying their skills for the U.S. Army in the European Theater, in the Pacific the U.S. Marine Corps unleashed their secret weapon – the Navajo Code Talkers. This complex language was well suited to the task, so much so that by the end of the war 400 Navajos had been assigned variously to the Third, Fourth, and Fifth Marine Divisions.

Usually they were split up into two-man teams, one on either end of a field telephone or walkie-talkie so they could transmit coordinates for artillery or air strikes, relay information on enemy positions, and provide other valuable intelligence without the Japanese being able to decipher the information. During the desperate fighting on Iwo Jima, the code talkers especially proved their worth when they relayed some 800 messages without error, including the one announcing the legendary flag raising on Mount Suribachi.

Creek, Choctaw, Hopi, Menominee, and Ojibwa code talkers answered the call as well. Whether in communications, or other assignments on land, at sea, or in the air, the American Indian carried on a proud warrior heritage in the hard-fought campaigns of World War II. When the guns fell silent, these veterans could return to their home secure in the knowledge that they had been valiant warriors and stalwart soldiers.

FOR FURTHER READING

Bernstein, Allison R., *American Indians and World War II: Toward a New Era in Indian Affairs.* Norman: University of Oklahoma Press, 1991.

Britten, Thomas A., *American Indians and World War I: At War and At Home.* Albuquerque: University of New Mexico Press, 1997.

Dunlay, Thomas W., *Wolves for the Blue Soldiers: Indian Scouts and Auxiliaries with the United States Army, 1860–90.* Lincoln: University of Nebraska Press, 1982.

Hauptman, Lawrence M., *Between Two Fires: American Indians in the Civil War.* New York: Free Press, 1996.

Left: A distinct overcoat with sharply pointed hood was specified in a circular issued on 11 August 1890 from the Headquarters of the U.S. Army. According to a description by artist Frederick Remington, this gave the scouts an appearance 'something between Russian Cossacks [sic] and Black Crooks'. Unique service guidons also were designated: the first type, specified in August 1890, consisted of a red rectangular background bearing 'two crossed arrows' and the words 'U.S. Scouts' above in a semicircle. A month later a modified form of this flag was prescribed, making it questionable whether the first version ever was produced. *(Richard LaMotte, C.D.G.)*

Above: The same 1890 circular specified a distinct uniform for Indian scouts. Among the items called for was a dress helmet with a long red and white horsehair plume and bands and cords of the same color combination. *(GS)*

Left: The mounted (cavalry) helmet plate bore crossed arrows, and the crossed arrow motif likewise appeared on the helmet side buttons. *(JO)*

Left: The officer who suggested the scout uniform, Lieutenant Edward Casey, felt that forage caps were unbecoming to Indians whose 'broad cheek bones and masses of hair' were better set off by hats. Once again, a singular item was adopted – a furfelt black 'fatigue hat' with a 3½ inch brim that was finished on the outer edge with three rows of stitching. The crown was domed, and rose 3½ inches. Worsted cords were decreed for the hat. *(SI)*

Left: The 1890 Indian scout worsted cords were similar to those adopted in 1858 for what has come to be known as the 'Hardee hat'. These were made up of a strand of white and a strand of scarlet, terminating in 1¼ inch tassels. Evidently there were at least two variations of this accessory, with the chief differences being the makeup of the tassels and the construction of the slide. *(JG)*

Lower left: Another element introduced by the 1890 circular was a set of crossed arrows 3 inches in length with the letters 'USS' above in 'nickel or some other white metal'. This insignia was attached to the hat by a stout pin. *(JO)*

Right: As of 1890, regulations called for Indian scout trouser stripes to be 1 inch wide with scarlet piping for sergeants and ½ inch wide with scarlet piping on each side for corporals. The shirt is the 1883 pattern that remained in use until the first years of the twentieth century. *(Photograph by Glen Swanson. JP)*

Left: In 1899, a new style of hat cord terminating in acorn devices was adopted for all enlisted men in the army. Subsequently, the Indian scouts were to obtain a cord following this design, which they wore at least through to the eve of World War I. *(KC)*

Bottom: The 1902 regulations ushered in a new full dress uniform with breast cord. This scarlet and white intermixed cord was made for Indians scouts. It resembled those produced for engineer enlisted personnel, but white was the predominant color for the scouts rather than the scarlet used for engineers. Such finery probably was rarely employed, and only two of these cords are known to exist. *(AHS)*

Below: A custom metal device probably made to ornament the schebraque of the Kiowa Indian scout Hunting Horse. *(JO)*

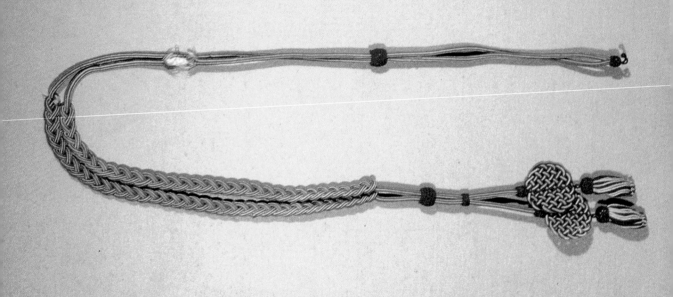

Right: In 1902, new uniform regulations swept away most of the old patterns of uniforms and insignia. A scout in the summer service dress of cotton khaki is depicted here with the chevrons of a lance corporal as authorized from 1903 through 1904. *(Richard Lamotte, C.D.G.)*

Below: With the new regulations, the bright crossed arrows eventually gave way to a subdued block 'USS' that was to be pinned on each side of the collar of the service uniform coat, and on the campaign hat. This custom collar and campaign hat insignia circa 1905 was for the Kiowa scout Hunting Horse. *(JO)*

Left and above: During World War I, several Choctaws served in the Thirty-sixth Infantry Division. Doughboys in this unit were distinguished by a shoulder sleeve insignia that, appropriately enough, was a light blue flint arrowhead with a 'T' in the center for Texas (although many of the men in this national guard outfit came from Oklahoma). Three of the Choctaw infantrymen in the Thirty-sixth were presented with the French *Croix de Guerre* for their heroic exploits. The US collar disk bearing the company letter was placed on the right side and the infantry collar disk with regimental number went on the left. *(Richard Lamotte, C.D.G.)*

Below: Two Apache scouts at Fort Huachuca, Arizona hold Springfield .30-06 bolt action rifles, the famed M-1 Garand not being issued generally prior to Pearl Harbor, when this picture was taken. The men are wearing enlisted overseas caps, olive drab wool trousers, and early versions of the so-called M1941 field jacket (PQD No. 20A olive drab field jacket). *(NA)*

Right: A lone Apache surveys the terrain at Fort Huachuca, Arizona, in about 1941. He is one of the last of his people to serve as a scout, a role that began soon after the Civil War. True to tradition, he appears on horseback, mounted on a McClellan saddle with a leather scabbard attached for his Springfield .30-06 rifle. *(NA)*

Below: On 6 August 1942, the First Special Service Force was authorized and, given the nature of the unit's mission, it seemed logical to assign the old Indian Scout insignia to the men of the 'Devil's Brigade'. Sheet brass disks were prescribed for enlisted men and a larger version was used by officers. Change 2 to Army Regulations dated 31 March 1944 discontinued this short-lived insignia. Later, when the Special Forces were established early in the Cold War era, crossed arrows were incorporated into the design of devices worn on the flash of the green beret. *(KC)*

Left: Almost one-fifth of the strength of the Forty-fifth Infantry Division, a unit distinguished by their 'Thunderbird' shoulder sleeve insignia, were American Indians. Depicted here is the 1943-pattern field uniform with M1 helmet, issued late in the war when the division had pushed into Germany in 1945. Veterans tended not to wear the shoulder sleeve insignia because it offered a bright red target for enemy snipers. *(Richard Lamotte, C.D.G.)*

Below: World War II shoulder sleeve insignia of the Forty-fifth Infantry Division. *(KC)*

Above: In the mid-to-late 1860s, cast-off Civil War clothing was used to outfit Indian scouts. The warrior-turned-scout posing with the rifle on his shoulder wears the 'bummer's' cap with stamped brass 1858-pattern cavalry insignia and 1858-pattern infantry frock coat. To his right, another man has adorned an 1858-pattern regulation enlisted hat with silver conchos and a feather. *(WSM)*

Right: Night Chief (left) and Man Who Left His Enemy Lying in Water posed for this photo circa 1870. Both were Pawnee scouts who, for the most part, eschewed any elements of military uniform, although they wear peace medals around their necks as symbols of allegiance to the 'Great White Father'. *(NSHS)*

Left: During the 1873 Lava Beds clash in Northern California against the Modocs, Warm Spring scouts from Oregon took to the field in support of the U.S. Army. Loakum Arnuk was among their number, seen here with a Spencer seven-shot carbine, and an M1839 belt plate and waist belt that he has elected to use as a sling to hold the cartridge box in place. An 1858-pattern regulation hat ornamented with stamped sheet brass insignia (placed askew contrary to regulations) appears on the protective lava rocks above him. *(NA)*

Left: In another image from the Lava Beds clash, several of the Warm Spring scouts have donned 1851-pattern sky-blue kersey enlisted dismounted greatcoats. They all wear the 1858-pattern soft furfelt hat. Spencer carbines dominate. *(NA)*

Right: Warm Spring scouts at the Lava Beds again have opted for the 1858-pattern hat, but their weapons also include a .50-70 Allin Conversion Springfield Rifle, which is evident in the left center of the photograph. *(NA)*

Below: In the years immediately following the Civil War, Navajos sometimes were recruited as scouts in New Mexico. This man may be one of them. He is armed with a percussion Colt revolver that has been converted to use metallic cartridges. *(BH)*

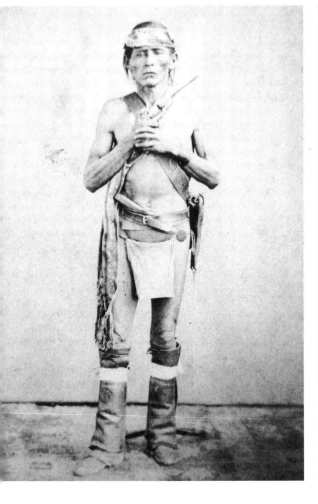

Above: Crow scout Bloody Knife would be killed at the Little Bighorn. Before his death, however, he was photographed wearing an 1874-pattern enlisted blouse complete with cavalry corporal's chevrons, and regulation sky-blue kersey trousers with a ½ inch yellow stripe down the outer seam. He is armed with a lever action 1873 Winchester. *(GS)*

Far left: In this August 1874 picture, Bloody Knife appears (left) with Lieutenant Colonel George Custer (center with rifle in hand). The scout has set aside more obvious military attire, and brandishes a heavy-caliber Sharps carbine. He has opted to use a 'fairweather christian' cartridge belt, popular among civilians and many soldiers at this time. *(GS)*

Left: In 1878 First Lieutenant Stephen W. Mills, Twelfth U.S. Infantry (front row on ground) commanded Company D, Indian Scouts, at Fort Apache, Arizona Territory. His men hold heavy .45-70 Springfield 'trapdoor' rifles. *(USAMHI)*

Lower left: First Lieutenant William Baird of the Sixth U.S. Cavalry (marked with 'X') and the Apache members of Company A, Indian Scouts, at Fort Apache in 1875. Tribal dress combined with bits and pieces of military uniforms, accoutrements, and government issue Springfield rifles made this group barely distinguishable from the enemy they pursued during the campaigns in the Southwest. *(NA)*

Below: Except for a government issue trapdoor rifle, Gar appeared in this 1878 study in the same basic dress as the Apaches he trailed. This situation was not unusual. Consequently, distinguishing friend from foe in the heat of combat presented a challenge to white troops. Gar was one of the mutineers from Company A, Sixth Cavalry, at the Battle of Cibecue, 29 August 1881. *(NA)*

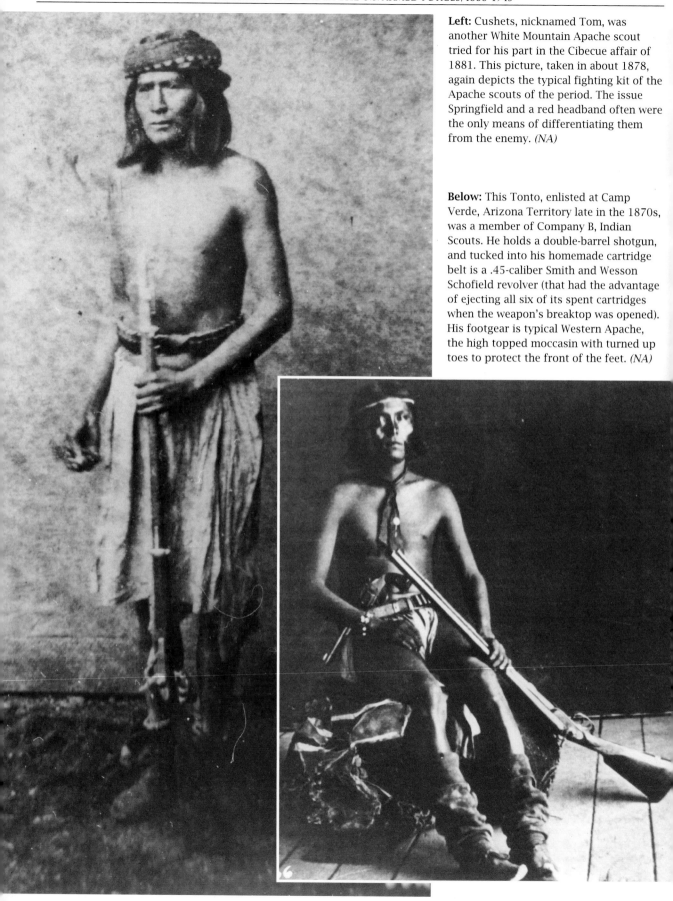

Left: Cushets, nicknamed Tom, was another White Mountain Apache scout tried for his part in the Cibecue affair of 1881. This picture, taken in about 1878, again depicts the typical fighting kit of the Apache scouts of the period. The issue Springfield and a red headband often were the only means of differentiating them from the enemy. *(NA)*

Below: This Tonto, enlisted at Camp Verde, Arizona Territory late in the 1870s, was a member of Company B, Indian Scouts. He holds a double-barrel shotgun, and tucked into his homemade cartridge belt is a .45-caliber Smith and Wesson Schofield revolver (that had the advantage of ejecting all six of its spent cartridges when the weapon's breaktop was opened). His footgear is typical Western Apache, the high topped moccasin with turned up toes to protect the front of the feet. *(NA)*

Above: Other members of B Company tended toward traditional Apache garb, although the seated man on the left wears the U.S. Army 1872-pattern pleated blouse. The man standing in the rear center is Mickey Free. *(NA)*

Right: Al Seiber once called Mickey Free 'half Mexican, half Irish and whole son of a bitch'. Despite this derisive description, Free proved valuable as an interpreter, serving for three and a half years with both First Lieutenant Britton Davis and Captain Emmet Crawford. He wears an 1885-pattern dark blue wool five-button enlisted blouse with first sergeant chevrons with its distinctive diamond showing faintly on the sleeve above the elbow. The boots are the 1876-pattern. *(AHS)*

Left: In this image taken in the mid-1880s, Brigadier General George Crook has dismounted from his mule 'Apache'. He is flanked by scouts Dutchy (left) and Al-che-say (right). Al-che-say wears an M1876 issue cartridge belt and an 1883-pattern field shirt. He was a respected 'Cayetero' leader and a Medal of Honor recipient, as were nine other Apaches who fought alongside George Crook in the 1872–73 campaign. *(NA)*

Left: Bakeitzogie (Yellow Coyote) was known variously to the whites as Dutchy or Dead Shot. He has opted to wear both a custom cartridge belt, and a regulation Mills cartridge belt with cast US buckle and brown canvas body that began to be issued in the early 1880s. *(NA)*

Opposite page, top: By 1880, First Lieutenant Charles Gatewood (in the large, non-regulation planter's hat) commanded Company A. Standing behind him is his chief of scouts and interpreter, Sam Bowman. The only unifying item in the group is the .45-70 Springfield rifle, although elements of regulation uniform are visible, such as the 1872-pattern infantry dress coat worn by the man wearing a light-colored civilian hat (front row center). *(NA)*

Opposite page, bottom: One of Gatewood's Apache scouts (back row, far right) in this 1883 image wears a summer helmet of the type that was sent to the Southwest on an experimental basis in the late 1870s, and adopted as official headgear in 1880. The crouching scout (front row left) wears an 1882-pattern campaign shirt with branch colored piping (either light blue for infantry or yellow for cavalry). *(NA)*

Left: During the Apache campaigns, German-born Al Seiber (front row seated) gained a reputation in his capacity as chief of scouts under General Crook. The Indian scouts in his charge are Tonto Apaches, who pose painted and stripped as was typical for war. The white man (center back) may be an official from Washington decked out in buckskin regalia to impress his friends in the East, although some sources identify him as 'Indian Mack'. *(NA)*

Left: Another atypical piece of headwear appears in this circa 1885 image of First Lieutenant Marion P. Maus (crouched on the right with a broadbrimmed non-regulation hat cavalierly pinned up on one side) and his Apache scouts. The man second front left wears an 1881-pattern enlisted infantry dress helmet with spike. The item probably was borrowed from a local foot soldier for this staged image. *(NA)*

Right: Tom Horn was another white who was hired during the Apache campaigns, for the most part as a mule packer but, according to his inflated autobiography, as a scout, interpreter, and more. Two of the scouts posing with him wear 1884-pattern gauntlets, and three have on regulation five-button blouses, including Mickey Free (seated to Horn's left) whose jacket bears the chevrons of a first sergeant. *(NA)*

Below: Many of the men of Company F, at San Carlos, Arizona Territory have opted for the five-button blouse, while some wear vests and other civilian items mixed with their Apache garb. *(NA)*

Above: White Mountain Apache Scouts of Company G around 1883. Except for the man standing at the left who has on a regulation blouse with corporal's chevrons, most of the unit seems little impressed with issue uniform items. Conversely, regulation M1876 cartridge belts and Springfield .45-70 rifles are the norm. *(USAMHI)*

Opposite page, top: 'Cut-Mouth' (seated in the center) was the first sergeant of Company A, as indicated by the three stripes with diamond above in this Christian Barthelmess photograph taken at Fort Apache around 1884. The man seated to the sergeant's right wears a traditional Apache cap, while several examples of issue cartridge belts can be seen. *(NA)*

Right: Once again, First Lieutenant Maus' scouts are captured by the camera, this time by Tombstone, Arizona, photographer C. S. Fly. Nearly all wear the five-button blouse, many with chevrons indicating their status as non-commissioned officers. Enlisted men from either the Fourth or Sixth U.S. Cavalry regiment are in the background. *(PS)*

Right: This warrior's outfit represents the common mixture of ancestral Apache trappings – including the bow, arrow, long loin cloth, and high-topped, turned-up-toes moccasins – with items provided by whites, most notably the dark blue wool 1883-pattern campaign shirt. *(PS)*

Below: While the bow and arrow could be repaired relatively easily, both Apache scouts and warriors had a preference for firearms, including the long-barreled U.S. Army model of the Colt single-action revolver. A brace of these are seen in the hands of this battle-ready subject, including one that was nickel plated. *(FHHM)*

Opposite page: Two White Mountain Apaches serving under Lieutenant David McDonald in the early 1880s dazzle the camera with colorful Native American and civilian attire. Only the Mills cartridge belt and the Springfield carbine are government issue. *(FHHM)*

89729

Above: The scout in the Apache-style headdress (far right) has strapped on a revolver in a civilian holster. However, his Mills cartridge belt with stamped brass buckle, five-button blouse, gauntlets, and high top boots (probably of the 1884 pattern) are regulation, as are many elements of the dress worn by this group of scouts in the mid-1880s. *(AHS)*

Left: Once more the Springfield (in this case a rifle with the M1879 rear sight) and the Mills belt with cast buckle are the only indications that Esh-kin-tsay-gizah is a scout rather than a member of Geronimo's or Victorio's bands. *(GS)*

Right: In the early 1880s, Lieutenant Mills' Apache Company A preferred light-colored cotton or canvas clothing with broadbrimmed light-colored hats, rather than military issue uniform articles. *(USAMHI)*

Right: Al-che-say holds the carbine version of the Springfield with the M1884 Buffington rear sight. His belt appears to be the M1885 woven carbine cartridge belt with leather tongue. *(GS)*

Opposite page, top: A sergeant from Company A circa 1885 opted for the blue wool enlisted five-button blouse with cavalry chevrons, although once again the trousers are of a lighter material than the issue sky-blue kersey. *(PS)*

Opposite page, bottom: In the final analysis, however, when combat erupted the Apache scouts might remove all the white man's trappings save issue cartridge belts and longarms, and go into battle in a simple loincloth, in the same way as did their foes. *(AHS)*

Above: Not all the scouts serving in the American Southwest were Apaches. Navajos continued to sign on in this capacity, as shown by these six men with Captain Allen Smith (center) of the Fourth U.S. Cavalry in 1881. Two men wear the 1874-pattern five-button blue wool enlisted blouse. Most carry .45-70 Springfield single-shot carbines, although the man on the far left and the one second from the right have experimental Ward-Burton bolt-action magazine arms, as does their officer. *(CBF)*

Right: Another group that served in the Southwest was the so-called Seminole–Negro scouts. All had African ancestry, but some also traced their heritage to certain Native American peoples who had been deported west of the Mississippi River from Florida and elsewhere. In this 1889 snapshot, six scouts stand at attention with a retired comrade, Dembo Factor (center with the white beard). Sky-blue kersey trousers, the five-button blue wool enlisted blouse, and 1883-pattern drab campaign hats provide a certain degree of uniformity. *(ITC)*

Top left: First Lieutenant Edward Casey of the Twenty-second Infantry (center foreground) was a strong advocate of regularization for the Indian scouts. Consequently, the Cheyennes in Troop A under his command turned out in complete government issue, as seen in this 1890 picture. All wear the 1889-pattern campaign hat, wool five-button blouse and medium blue kersey trousers, and use the standard cavalry saddle gear with gray horse blanket. *(CBF)*

Left: Here Casey's scouts have dismounted at their camp along the Yellowstone River near Fort Keogh, Montana, and stand to horse, their M1885 McClellan saddles clearly showing. Attached to one saddle (far left) is a brass throated carbine boot that held the .45-70 Springfield when the rider was on horseback. *(NA)*

Above: In their camp, men of Casey's unit are less regulated, some wearing civilian shirts or the 1883-pattern blue wool issue campaign shirt. A few have cravats or scarves, and most have modified the crowns of their 1889-pattern drab campaign as a statement of individuality. *(CBF)*

Left: The Cheyenne scout White Moon has discarded his 1889-pattern campaign hat for a rather ornate, soft civilian cowboy hat. However, the remainder of his rig is regulation, including the 1885-pattern mounted reinforced trousers and the half flap holster with its embossed 'US' that was adopted in 1881. *(CBF)*

Top right: During the Ghost Dance in the winter of 1890, the final tragic effort by the Sioux to call back their dead warriors from the grave to drive the white man from their land, Casey's men were mobilized for duty. They make their way to Pine Ridge Agency, South Dakota wearing the special hooded overcoats that their commanding officer had proposed in lieu of the standard kersey model with capes issued to regular troops. *(CBF)*

Right: Lieutenant William Taylor's company of Oglala Sioux Scouts also went to Pine Ridge. Most of the men have been issued with the 1879-pattern muskrat fur cap. Lieutenant Taylor is standing on the far right of this shot. *(GS)*

Right: Lieutenant Taylor (seated center) flanked by seven of his scouts on 19 January 1891 at Pine Ridge. Two of his men at the left and the one seated beside him have stuffed the legs of their trousers into 1887-pattern boots, while all carry Colt revolvers in M1881 holsters and cradle Springfield carbines with M1884 Buffington rear sights. *(NA)*

Opposite page, top: In late November of 1890, First Lieutenant Sydney Cloman recruited a company of Oglala Sioux at Pine Ridge Reservation. Here the men gather round to consider enlisting. *(USAMHI)*

Opposite page, center: A number of warriors were persuaded to join Cloman. They have received muskrat caps, and carry carbines, many of which have the detachable sheet metal front side hood that was approved in 1888. *(NSHS)*

Opposite page, bottom: Civilians, scouts, soldiers and Sioux are gathered at the Pine Ridge Agency store. The man standing on the porch (third from the left) wears the 1890 Indian scout hat with crossed arrows insignia. He is a sergeant as indicated by the 1 inch white stripe bordered in scarlet and the white chevrons with red chainstitching. *(NSHS)*

Top right: Woman's Dress, a Lakota stationed at Fort Robinson, Nebraska in the early 1890s, has fastened the Indian scout insignia adopted in 1890 to the front of his headgear, which is a civilian slouch hat rather than regulation issue. He wears cavalry sergeant's chevrons on his five-button blouse, which he has further customized by adding a small U.S. flag to the left breast. *(GS)*

Right: Although in 1890 special overcoats for Indian scouts were prescribed, these garments, like so much of their distinct regalia, probably saw limited use. The Apache sergeant on the right wears a standard medium blue wool kersey enlisted greatcoat of the type made from the mid-1880s through the late 1890s. He has removed the cape, but added pockets with flaps as a non-regulation modification. His chevrons are white with red chainstitching, as are those of the first sergeant next to him. First Sergeant Cut-Mouth (seated), wears a Medal of Honor although he was not one of the ten Apache scouts to be so recognized for valor. Perhaps he borrowed the item from Sergeant Rowdy, who received his medal as a result of an engagement in 1890. *(USAMHI)*

Company of Apache Indian Scouts

Left: Two members of the Indian scouts stationed at Fort Apache, Arizona circa 1890 (front row center and second from left), have been issued with the 1884-pattern five-button blouse with three external slash pockets. These garments did not see widespread use. *(FHHM)*

Above: Company A at Fort Reno, Oklahoma, was manned by Southern Cheyennes. Most of them have accepted 1889-pattern campaign hats, which they have altered in a variety of ways to provide distinctiveness, although the first sergeant in the center has opted for a black slouch hat. *(NA)*

Left: By 1893 the Apache scouts at San Carlos Reservation in Arizona had been provided with the special red and white guidon advocated by Lieutenant Casey. This is evident on the far left of the formation consisting of twelve privates, a corporal, a sergeant and the first sergeant, along with a civilian interpreter and the commanding officer, First Lieutenant Clarence E. Dentler. *(AHS)*

Above: Several of the men of Company A at Fort Reno have set aside campaign hats in favor of 1880-pattern summer helmets, which stand out even in this faded print from the 1890s. *(USAMHI)*

Left: Arapaho George Little Bear was a trumpeter with Company A of the Indian Scouts. An 1880-pattern white summer helmet is next to him in this circa 1895 photograph, one indication of the increasing trend toward uniformity comparable to regular army troops. The instrument is the standard brass 'F' trumpet prescribed for foot soldiers, although the scouts were a mounted unit. The worsted bugle cords probably were yellow, however, as this was the color for cavalry. *(NA)*

In 1891 the Secretary of War directed that Native Americans be recruited into the regular army, either in Troop L in the First through Eighth U.S. Cavalry regiments, or segregated into Company I in a number of infantry regiments. This Apache of the Twelfth Infantry at Mount Vernon Barracks, Alabama, wears the standard garrison uniform, including M1885 waist belt with cast brass rectangular plate bearing a 'US' within and raised oval. *(USAMHI)*

Opposite page, top: First Sergeant Meat of Company A, Southern Cheyenne Indian Scouts at Fort Reno, Indian Territory, posed with his family circa 1890 holding an 1880-pattern enlisted sun helmet. His three stripes with a diamond indicate his rank, as does the 1 inch leg stripe on the outer seams of his trousers. *(USAMHI)*

Above: These Apache members of Company I, Twelfth U.S. Infantry, wear the brown canvas 1884-pattern fatigue uniform with 1889-pattern campaign hat, garb that was somewhat more suitable to the hot, humid climate of the South than the dark blue wool garrison uniform. *(USAMHI)*

Left: Captain Henry A. Green, at the front of the column in an officer's 1892-pattern blouse and forage cap, commands Company I, Twentieth Infantry, whose men were Native Americans. The foot soldiers, turned out at Camp Poplar River, Montana, are all in field kit, including the canvas M1888 blanket bag (knapsack), as well as the haversack and canteen. *(MHS)*

Left: First Sergeant Chester Arthur adopted his non-Indian name from the president of the United States. He was the top soldier of Company I, Twentieth U.S. Infantry as indicated by the white chevrons with lozenge on the sleeves of his five-button blouse and the insignia on his forage cap. He wears a vest, which was allowed by regulations but, as it was not an issue item, was bought by the individual soldier. *(MHS)*

Right: Brule Sioux foot soldiers in Company I, Sixteenth U.S. Infantry, were posted to Fort Douglas, Utah Territory. They stand in front of their barracks at parade rest with their .45-70 rifles. Both the 1889-pattern leggings and the campaign hat adopted in the same year are evident. *(LDS)*

Right: Apaches from Company I, Ninth U.S. Infantry served in the Southwest for a few years in the early 1890s. One wears the 1889-pattern forage cap with crossed rifle insignia indicating company and regiment; the rest have on the 1889-pattern drab campaign hat. A sergeant and a corporal (right) wear white chevrons, the branch color adopted for infantry in 1884. All have purchased bandannas, an accessory that was never issued but occasionally bought by the soldiers from their meager pay. *(AMWH)*

Left: In a less formal pose, Sioux doughboys of the Sixteenth Infantry still cut a martial figure in their well tailored post-1884 dark blue wool five-button blouses and medium blue kersey 1885-pattern trousers. Non-commissioned officers are set apart by trouser stripes (½ inch wide for corporals and 1 inch wide for sergeants and the first sergeant) as well as by appropriate chevrons in white. *(LDS)*

Below: Here the Sioux of the Sixteenth Infantry wear the 1879-pattern muskrat fur cap, 1889-pattern medium blue kersey overcoat with dark blue lined cape, and 1889-pattern brown canvas leggings as their winter service uniform. *(NSHS)*

Above: Crow warriors turned troopers in Company L, First Cavalry, fall out in their finery – the 1881-pattern dress helmet with dark yellow horsetail plume and cords and the 1887-pattern dark blue wool cavalry dress coat trimmed in yellow with gold lace chevrons. *(NA)*

Opposite page, top: With his saber at the ready, its leather knot hanging downward, this Crow trooper of the First Cavalry is astride his government issue mount which he controls by means of the M1874 'Shoemaker' bit and reins. He has coiled his picket rope loosely to the pommel of his McClellan saddle that rests atop a gray saddle blanket with yellow stripe. *(NA)*

Right: The First Cavalry's Crow troopers at saber drill, with the M1859 light cavalry saber drawn. The men ride on McClellan saddles, and at least one of them has on an M1885 carbine sling. *(NA)*

Above: First Lieutenant Samuel Robertson, in an officer's 1872-pattern forage cap, speaks to one of the men in Company L, First U.S. Cavalry. The Crow trooper has substituted leggings for his standard boots. He wears a Mills belt bandoleer style, and has added a light colored bandanna to his outfit. *(USAMHI)*

Left: Putting aside their 1881-pattern dress helmets for forage caps, two Brule Sioux with Company L, Sixth U.S Cavalry, wear their 1887-pattern enlisted cavalry full dress uniforms. The man on the left is a trumpeter, indicated not only by his bugle, but also by yellow worsted 'herringbones' on the chest of his coat. There also would be a pair of double ½ inch stripes of yellow facing material along the outer seams of his kersey trousers. *(AMWH)*

Above: The 1889-pattern forage caps of these men bear the stamped sheet brass crossed sabers and the number '4' and the letter 'L' as appropriate for American Indians serving with Troop L of the Fourth Cavalry in the early 1890s. *(PS)*

Left: In the early 1890s two unidentified members of Company L, Sixth U.S. Cavalry, went to famed photographer O.S. Goff to be immortalized. Their non-regulation neckerchiefs became a cliché in Hollywood depictions, although in reality were rarely worn. *(GS)*

Left: Enlisted men of Troop L, Seventh U.S. Cavalry (predominantly from the Kiowa and Comanche peoples) at Fort Sill, Oklahoma, wear the 1895-pattern forage cap. *(NA)*

Opposite page, bottom: In late 1898, Company A of the Apache Scouts was commanded by First Lieutenant George A. Pritchard (far left with his horse turned sideways). He wears the 1895-pattern officer's blouse. *(USAMHI)*

Below: Company A's Apache scouts gather at Camp Grant, Arizona Territory, after their Saturday morning inspection on 12 November 1898. They all carry the Krag .30 caliber carbine that began to replace the .45-70 Springfield in the mid-1890s. *(USAMHI)*

Left: Two Apache scouts and a white trooper at Fort Huachuca, Arizona Territory, photographed around the turn of the century. The scout on the left wears the 1890-pattern nickel crossed arrows insignia. The man on the right is Private Major whose son, William, would later serve as a scout at the same military post. *(USAMHI)*

Right: In this circa 1905 image, Seminole-Negro Indian scouts appear in the dress uniform adopted at the end of 1902. Instead of the new 'USS' collar insignia prescribed in that year, all display standard enlisted 'US' gilt insignia on their collars and caps. *(SISCA)*

Right: Three Seminole Indian scouts at Fort Clark, Texas, present the company's distinctive red and white guidon with bow and arrows in the center and the words 'US Scouts' above and 'Dept of Texas' below, in this 1910 picture. All their kit is regulation, including the gauntlets. *(KM)*

Above: The entire troop of Seminole Indian scouts appears in another photograph taken at Fort Clark, Texas, circa 1910. All wear the 1902-pattern campaign hat. *(USAMHI)*

Left: The enlistment of Apache scouts had waned by the early 1900s, but the 1916 Punitive Expedition launched against Pancho Villa in Mexico brought about a brief resurgence in their employment. One of Brigadier General John 'Black Jack' Pershing's finest wears a head scarf rather than the campaign hat, and Apache hightop moccasins instead of army issue canvas puttees and leather shoes. The remainder of his kit essentially is regulation, including the 1911-pattern olive drab shirt and the cartridge belt with suspenders. *(NA)*

Opposite page, top: Apache Indian scouts with Pershing's forces during the Punitive Expedition have donned the 1911-pattern 'Montana Peak' campaign hat and the olive drab wool field uniform, much as their counterparts in the cavalry, infantry, and artillery did during this excursion into Mexico. *(NA)*

Opposite page, bottom: In 1918, Indian scouts stand in front of the adjutant's office at Fort Apache, Arizona. They are wearing 1907-pattern leggings and the olive drab uniform, except Corporal C.F. Josh (far left), who wears denim trousers. The corporal, along with two men toward the center, Privates Jesse Palmer and Tea Square, have pinned 'USS' insignia to the crown of their hats. *(FHHM)*

Left: During World War I, thousands of American Indians served in the military, both in the United States and abroad. One of those who went overseas was Alphonse Bear Ghost, a Lakota. Each gold chevron on the lower left sleeve indicates six months' service in Europe – a total of a year and a half. *(WHM)*

Right: These four doughboys of Company G, Thirteenth U.S. Infantry, wear the 1911-pattern 'Montana Peak' campaign hat. Two of the men were Comanche, one a Southern Cheyenne, and one an Aleut. *(WHM)*

Below: Paiute Robert Dodd (back row, middle) displays an overseas' stripe above the left cuff of his olive drab stand collar coat of the pattern first issued in 1911, and a wound stripe above his right cuff. *(WHM)*

Opposite page: Winnebago Sam Thundercloud also was wounded. A member of Company D, 128th Infantry, Thundercloud wears the service or overseas cap that was adopted in lieu of the campaign hat shortly after the Americans came to Europe in 1917. The leg wraps also were a replacement for the leggings issued before the war. Shoulder sleeve insignia likewise represented a wartime innovation, with Private Thundercloud's being an unusually large version of the red arrow of the Thirty-second Division. It appears that the cross bar is white rather than the traditional red. Moreover, the arrow is worn at a downward angle, rather than the more common vertical with point up toward the shoulder. *(WHM)*

Right: By the early 1900s, most of the few remaining scouts were Apaches. One exception was Kiowa Sergeant I-See-O, who was carried on the muster rolls as a sergeant major in deference to his long, honorable service. In this candid portrait taken around 1925, he wears the stand collar olive drab wool service coat, first prescribed in 1911 but whose many modifications included the bright buttons (seen here) introduced in 1924. All versions of these coats were designed to have disks on the collars to indicate branch and unit affiliation. No crossed arrow versions were mentioned in regulations, therefore the sergeant wears an enlisted Quartermaster Corps insignia. *(NA)*

Right: During the August 1941 Louisiana maneuvers, Sergeant Washington Mihecoby, a Comanche codetalker serving with the U.S. Army Fourth Division, acts as an operator for the BD-72 telephone switchboard. This piece of equipment was a mainstay for regimental headquarters, division artillery, and similar sized units. He wears blue denim army fatigue trousers and an overseas cap. *(HF)*

Above: A Comanche code talker serving as a U.S. Army Signal Corpsman ascends a pole at Camp Gordon, Georgia, in February 1942, as part of his duties as a lineman. His "climbing gaffs" appear to be one-piece herringbone twill coveralls. *(HF)*

Right: In the early 1940s, Kiowa scout Tsain-tonkee (Hunting Horse) was trotted out for a publicity photograph. Either the Fort Sill Museum loaned him items from its collection, or the old soldier had obtained 19th-century uniform components, such as the 1858-pattern hat and what appears to be an 1890-pattern Indian scout dress coat, in some other way. Perhaps the latter rare item dated from his days on active duty, which began with his first enlistment in early 1875. *(JO)*

Opposite page, top: Sioux enlisted men show an elder a .50 caliber machine gun sometime during the summer of 1942. The men are members of the Fourth U.S. Cavalry Mechanized Regiment, as indicated by the distinctive metal unit insignia on their overseas caps consisting of a yellow shield with pale blue on which an arrow, bayonet, and saber are superimposed. *(NA)*

Opposite page, bottom: Sioux men prepare to raise the colors prior to a traditional Sun Dance. They wear breeches and leather riding boots indicating that they are cavalrymen, although their unit – the Fourth U.S. Cavalry – had abandoned horses for motorized vehicles by this time (August 1942). *(NA)*

Left: In 1943, James Collins Ottipoby, a Comanche from Oklahoma, was the first American Indian chaplain to be commissioned in the U.S. Army. A Methodist minister, the silver Latin cross on his khaki shirt collar indicates his status as a Christian chaplain, while the silver bar on the right denotes his rank as a first lieutenant. *(NA)*

Below: Dan Waupoose, a Menomini who enlisted in the U.S. Navy, wears sailor's dungarees with a feathered headdress, and carries a Springfield .30-caliber bolt-action rifle and its long bayonet for an unlikely combat outfit cobbled together for a 1943 public relations image. *(NA)*

Right: In this 1943 picture, nineteen-year-old Private First Class Ira Hayes, a Pima from Arizona, attends U.S. Marine Corps paratrooper school. Hayes, who was stateside for training, wears the marine intermediate weather summer service dress, a far cry from the combat gear he would be dressed in when photographed with other Leathernecks at the famous Iwo-Jima flag raising. *(NA)*

Left: Marine Privates First Class Alec E. Nez (left) and William D. Yazie, were two Navajos assigned to the Marine Corps Pacific Division in Honolulu during World War II. They were crack shots, as indicated by the marksmanship medals pinned on the coat style khaki shirts that formed part of the intermediate weather summer service dress. *(NA)*

Left: Cousins Preston and Frank Toledo were members of the famed U.S. Marine Corps Navajo Code Talkers. They both wear the forest green garrison cap with bronze eagle, globe, and anchor insignia on the left side. *(NA)*

Above: On Guam were Privates First Class George H. Kirk (left) and John V. Goodluck (right), Navajo signalmen assigned to the Pacific Theater of Operations during World War II. While both the standard M1 steel helmet and the venerable U.S. Marine Corps campaign hats are evident, these Leathernecks preferred the soft herringbone twill utility cap. *(NA)*

Left: These Navajo Marine signalmen have replaced their stateside garb with combat gear for their duty at Bouganville. The sage green 1942-pattern utility uniform is worn by all the group save one, who has opted for the 1944-pattern camouflaged herringbone twill uniform. The same man holds a Thompson submachine gun, while the rest of his comrades favor the M1 Garand. *(NA)*

Right: Three American Indian women reservists with the U.S. Marine Corps wear the forest green female winter service dress uniform designed early in World War II by Manibocher. The cap cords were scarlet. From left to right, Minnie Spotted Wolf (Blackfoot), Celia Mix (Potawatomi), and Viola Chipman (Chippewa) were the trio in this 1943 group portrait. *(NA)*

Left: Olive drab wool coat style shirts and trousers were mainstays in the European Theater of Operations, as worn by First Lieutenant Ernest Childers, a Creek who destroyed two German machine gun nests in Italy to earn a Medal of Honor. He is being congratulated by Lieutenant General Jacob Devers, who wears an officer's stylish 'pinks and greens' (August 1944). *(NA)*

Right: First Lieutenant Woody Cochran, a Cherokee from Oklahoma, served in the Army Air Force as a B-17 pilot against the Japanese, as indicated by the Nambu pistol with holster and flag he displays as souvenirs. In this 1943 photograph he wears the khaki trousers and coat style shirt often donned by aviators in the Pacific. *(NA)*